# Cleaning The Duck

# Cleaning
# The Duck

*Tsaurah Litzky*

Bowery Books
Bowery Poetry Series #10

YBK Publishers
New York

Please direct all inquiries to:
Editors, Bowery Books, 310 Bowery, New York, NY 10012
Email - Bowerybooks1@gmail.com

Bowery Books
Editors Bob Holman and Marjorie Tesser

ISBN 978-1-936411-10-8
Library of Congress Control Number 2011919085

Manufactured in the United States of America for distribution in North and South America or in the United Kingdom or Australia when distributed elsewhere.

Cover image by Tsaurah Litzky.
Author photograph by Nathan Versace

Bowery Books, the imprint of Bowery Arts + Science, a non-profit cultural organization, is grateful for the assistance we receive from individual donors, foundations and government arts agencies. This publication is made possible with public funds from The New York State Council on the Arts, a state agency, and from the National Endowment for the Arts. We are grateful also for assistance from the Council for Literary Magazines and Presses.

Bowery Books are published in affiliation with YBK Publishers, Inc., 39 Crosby Street, New York, NY 10013, whose publisher, Otto Barz, is the inspiration for this series. With thanks to Bill Adler.

*This book is dedicated to*

## Ruth Levin Litzky
1918-1999

and

## Jerry Litzky
1919-2011

# *Acknowledgements*

Heartfelt Thanks to Marjorie Tesser, Bob Holman, Danny Shot, Steve Cannon, Steve Dalachinsky, Jossy Muhleisen, R. C., Carol Wiersbicki, Rob Stupay, the Litzkys of Saverna Park, Ursula Clark, Nancy Mercado, Ethan Cornell, and Noah Cornell.

"Utopia Poem" appeared in *A Gathering Of The Tribes*, issue 12. "Blake Haunts Me" appeared in *Bowery Women*. "I am the Statue of Liberty" appeared in the *New York Times*. "Enid Ascends" appeared in *Long Shot*, volume 27. "Gitmo" appeared in *Curare*, volume 9. "I Love you, I.B. Singer" and "Easter" appeared in *Flying Fish, vol.3., Brevitas – Festival Of the Short Poem*, which inspired many of the poems here which are fourteen lines or less.

# Contents

# Cleaning
# The Duck

# Easter

*(for R.C.)*

6am Easter day
sitting at the kitchen table
filing my nails
with a worn emery board,
it's supposed to be spring,
but steam still hisses in the pipes,
the resurrection and the life,
vanished friends rustle
like leaves,
my eyes swell with memory,
blue blood of morning
rises in my veins,
good old sun pours clear light
into my tea,
future is a blossoming tree,
sea-saw life, please keep
rocking me, rocking me,
rocking me.

## Late Spring

Cherry blossoms open pink as labia
on this quiet Brooklyn street,
green blades feather out into leaves,
a sign finally, this long winter has passed,
my crazy heart buzzes up like a bee.

# The Poetry Workshop

I wake up so early, dawn just breaking outside my window,
I'm eager for poetry, eager for wings to take me
out of myself,
I want to write like I think breathe come,
I want to kiss Walt Whitman's thumb.

I dress carefully, wear my favorite clothes.

On the subway, the C train,
I travel to the unknown,
the homeless man across from me rubs his bone,
I pretend he is Orpheus playing the flute,
I pretend he is the God of Poetry, maybe he is.

The train stops at 116th Street, too soon.
I am frightened, will I to try to play it cool
while inside I'm a griddle sizzling to fry,
will I show off like I did in grade school,
desperate for attention, raising my hand so much
the other kids hated me.

I walk up the subway stairs and I'm in a far country,
mysterious, exotic, in the window of the bodega
the only fruits I recognize are coconuts.

Cars brake too fast for the light,
parrots shriek in the trees
the questing drums call to me,
I turn the corner on 115th Street,
walk down a street filled with spears.
I go up the library steps, open the door,
I am here.

# Julia

While waiting under the big clock at Penn Station
to meet my seventeen-year-old niece,
her train is thirty minutes late,
I remind myself not to hang on her,
not to let her catch me looking at her,
she has my mother's face but
has been spared the family nose,
I won't let her know how much I love her,
how much her visits mean to me,
I'll model myself after Auntie Mame,
*toujours gai, toujours gai,*
but when I see her
coming up the stairs,
grinning at me through her braces,
my heart leaps up into my throat
and there it stays, there it stays.

# Deliverance

On the Amtrak
late at night
on my way back from Maryland
where I went for the family seder,
the waning moon
I see out the train window
has a white beard of cloud,
I think of Moses
leading me though the
deserts of Pennsylvania, New Jersey,
back to New York City,
back to my freedom,
my sparse white room,
my writing table.

# I Am The Statue of Liberty

I am the Statue of Liberty,
my girdle curdled by partisan politics,
my hem ripped by the patriot act
but despite recent events
my intent remains intact,
to embody the ideal of liberty
in society with dignity and heart.
My crown is still on my head,
my libido is not dead,
I want to mate with the Golden Gate
and birth renewed civil liberties
so once again America will be
*land of the brave, home of the free.*

# Enid Ascends

*(for Enid Dame*
*1943–2003)*

Enid is reading the newspapers while
Donald eats a poppy seed bagel with salted butter.
Donald likes salt.
*There is more famine in Somalia,* she tells Donald,
*They bombed two synagogues in Istanbul,*
She reads on, *Bush has ordered six new cowboy hats*
*and can't find time to visit families*
*of soldiers killed in Iraq and Oh no!*
*they may set Milosovic free.*
*Please clear the breakfast dishes from the table, Donald.*
*I need to write a poem.*

Enid shakes the sky,
a rain of commas falls down like crescent moons,
Enid knows when to punctuate,
how to put each word in the right place,
she knows when a line is ripe,
how to pluck it
from the tree of life,
because Enid is the Queen of the Ripe,
of the place beyond laughter,
of the Stone Shekina and the perfect purple plum.

Enid is walking Brighton Beach
on a cold December afternoon
as the sun sets filling the sky behind the ocean
with the ruby breath of lovers.
Enid wakes at dawn, opens the window,
climbs out the fire escape,
she likes to carol with the early birds,
the sea gulls, the Brooklyn sparrows,
while high above, Lilth dances around the morning sun,
arms and legs twirling in the winds of creation.

Lilth reaches an opal hand down to Enid,
she grasps it, ascends, still wearing
the old, faded pink rayon slip she likes to sleep in,
the slip ripped at the hem, that reminds her of her mother.

In the afterlife, Enid visits Ethel Rosenberg.
They share an apple as they sit at the table
in Ethel's kitchen in the clouds,
Ethel has sliced the apple,
put it in a porcelain bowl between them.
Enid reaches for a slice of apple.
*You were born too soon,* she says to Ethel.
*You are right*, says Ethel and sighs
*but you*, she tells Enid,
*were born at the right time.*

## Blake In Amsterdam

Blake haunts me in a bed
in a room on
Grote Bieckerstraadt,
Blake calls me names:
snol, viswisf, verloren ziel,
gekke vrow,
*(harlot, fishwife, lost soul,*
*crazy woman),*
Blake haunts me in Dutch,
When I ask him - *Master William,*
*Where did you learn Dutch?*
He says, *in the spirit world, ninny girl,*
*you will know all languages,*
*everything is revealed,*
*you sleep wrapped in the tissue of dawn,*
*wake holding the reins of the sun.*

*No need to push your titties*
*out the top of a corset,*
*or jump on the bar and lift*
*your petticoats up,*
*in your earthly life, you will never get enough,*
*Na, na, na, nay, nay, na, na-na-na-nay-nay-nay*

*You want to catch the truth*
*like a beam of light*
*between your legs,*
*try as you will to use your sex like a crutch,*
*in the earthly world you will never get enough.*
*Hear me, ninny girl,*
*no matter how you shimmy and shake*
*yours are nay the hips that rock*
*the cradle of creation,*
*na, na, na, nay- nay-nay,*
*in your earthly life you will never get enough.*

## from Haikus Somehow Involving Water

### River View

thirty years
I climb these worn stairs,
my life currents idle by
or rush like wild prayer

### Washing Dishes

washing the dishes
my fingers swim like fishes
in the churning sea

### No Panties

beads of sweat cool my thighs,
no panties under my dress
on the hottest day of July

# Cleaning The Duck

It was a mallard Alex felled with a shot
in the swamp by the pine woods,
it wasn't dead so he wrung its neck and
gave it to Margo for dinner.
She put it in the refrigerator next to the milk carton,
there it was when we opened the door,
a fat duck, the neck folded futile as an empty sleeve
against the plump breast.
We put it on the table, I tried to cut off a wing,
hard to saw through bone, black blood on my fingers,
Anger! Tearing! Crack! The wing broke free,
spread out arms-length, long-feathered, phosphorescent,
gray as a storm, the underside of the wing so white it
could have shamed a pearl,
I sawed off the other wing,
Margo took one side, I the other,
we pulled the feathers out,
it was easy, they didn't make a sound,
we put them and the wings in a
brown paper bag from the A&P,
the job was done down to the soft down,
silky, fine as the hair of a newborn.
I took up the knife and with one sharp chop,
severed the head,
the room crowded with eagles beating their wings.
I cut off the tail, the entrails poured out like a waterfall,
Margo took a wooden spoon, scooped out the excrement,
the intestine; smells spread out covering us,
mildew, pus, sweat, earth, yeast, rust,
then with the knife I cut the chest,
separated the flaps of breast,
the lungs opened out like morning sunrise,
blue sky fading pink, rose, red, ruby, gold,

the heart of fire, the heat of birth,
the ribs reaching out with shy baby fingers.

Later we cooked the duck, it tasted like chocolate.

# Desire

Desire is a tricky web,
it catches me inside my head,
wraps tight around my legs,
cripples me with longing,
I start to write poems to you
but the words get
stuck in my throat
and I end up quacking
like a duck
afloat on murky waters.

# She Likes Me

I'm eating breakfast with my father in his new home
in a condo development for senior citizens.
*She likes me*, he says, as he digs into the container
of Breakstone's Lox and Cream Cheese Spread
with his spoon, since it doesn't do any good,
I no longer tell him I can't stand it when he
eats straight from the container like an animal,
*Who likes you?* I ask, he swallows,
*the one upstairs on the second floor,*
*the one over there,*
he gestures over his shoulder with the spoon.
*How do you know?* I ask,
he speaks even though he is chewing with his mouth full,
*I know,* he says, *she always gives me the big hello.*
I say, *That doesn't prove anything,*
*maybe she is just a very friendly person.*
He snaps back, *At eighty-nine years old*
*you know a few things.*
I want to tell him be sure and get a pre-nup,
I don't. I ask, *Is she on a walker too?*
*Nah,* he says, kvelling, smiling proudly,
*She drives an S.U.V.*

# May Day

I listen to the McNeil-Lehrer report
while I prepare my evening meal,
soup from the can and a slice of rye bread,
I bring my food to the table
during the silence when
they show the pictures
of the ten soldiers killed today
in Afghanistan and Iraq.
Lehrer begins his goodnight chatter,
my spoon hitting the side of the porcelain bowl
sounds like a shovel hitting a metal casket,
I can't eat my soup; it's turned to blood,
my bread to ashes.

# I Love You, Isaac Bashevis Singer

I love you I. B. Singer,
I love your lusty widows,
frizzed hair piled up
on their heads like
bunches of nesting spiders,
I love you I. B. Singer,
fiddler of my heart.

I put five sugars in my tea
and let you take me
to a turn of the century
café in Prague,
under my red velvet dress
I am wearing a corset
that makes my breasts
look like perfect apples,
and when you send a
suitor to my table,
an ersatz count, with a
mustache like a walrus,
who says he is a
friend of Kafka's,
he tells me my smile
is as full of mystery
as the new moon.

I love you I. B. Singer,
I love your Bessie Popkins
and your Bambergs,
your wild Broadway with the smells
of softened summer asphalt,
gasoline, rotten fruit,
and the excrement of dogs.
I grasp my pocketbook tightly
and walk into your world.

I look through your kaleidoscope eyes,
old as the Jewish exile,
and see vanished all-night cafeterias
where obscure writers
with ragged cuffs scribble
out their days on napkins
stained with butter and honey made
by the magic bees of Lublin.
Because of you, I. B. Singer,
I believe in luck and all superstitions,
I believe in demons and
climbing up the highest tree
in the forest
so I can better see the night,
I listened when you said
the power of darkness is like a monkey,
it mimics the light,
the dead, you told me,
don't know they are dead
and the living don't know
they are alive,
so laugh, dance, cry
and remember all philosophies
are meaningless.

I love you, I.B. Singer,
you made me desire
to make seven mile steps,
to take wine from the wall,
O, my vineyard word-wizard scribe
with your candles, cabbalists,
cuckolds, your crows in a pie,
your vision sharper than the moyhl's knife,
I love you, I.B. Singer, my spirit-pipe,
you are the kerchief of my life.

# No Sun

August,
gray day,
oppressive heat,
no sun, thunder!
Above the clouds
the newly dead,
blinded by the
white light,
howl,
humbled,
knock heads,
stumble.

## Alianthus

Out from the root
the alianthus,
shiny and quixotic as love,
pushes up between the cracks
in the pavement to branch up
and flower along the fire escape

Among the chips of glass and broken bottles
caught between the toes of the big weed,
the light changes from green to yellow
to brown like leaves,
fumes from passing cars mix with exhaust
from buses idling by the curb,
hot air steams up from the pavement in waves,
vapors, luminous lakes of air,
whole worlds flicker and shimmer
like fish in a lagoon.

When I close my eyes, I can
almost see far below the water
the diamond city I came to find
and under that, the bedrock,
a dense white stone opaque as anger.

If only I could find my way back,
through the shattered souls
cigarette butts and twisted days
to the path, the path that creeps like ailanthus
down through the weary streets
and opens, finally, into the bridge,
that will take me home.

# Lapsang Souchong

Lapsang Souchong was your favorite tea,
you showed me how to brew it how you liked it,
strong enough to knock down a wall,
you showed me other things,
how to find my clitoris, how to bake a pie in a hubcap,
how to throw the I Ching, how to roll marijuana cigarettes
while barreling eighty miles an hour down the highway in our
    VW bus

You showed me the Rio Grande,
the Sangre Del Christo mountains,
a purple path up beyond the clouds,
when you showed me the desert,
I didn't like it, it was too silent, too still,
I wanted the ocean, the clash of the waves,
the pull of the tides, maybe that was the problem.

The obituaries Richard sent from New Mexico
said at the time of your death you were
working on a novel about your days in New York,
that was when I knew you were thinking about me.
I always wanted to see you again,
show you my hair was still thick,
my waist twenty- four inches,
I wanted you to see how far I have come,
how well I have done with nothing,
now your ashes rest near your house in Buena Vista
while I wander through concrete canyons
looking for your shadow.

Today, your birthday, I threw the I Ching,
the hexagram I got was Oppression,
the image read *There is no water in the lake:*
*the image of exhaustion. Thus the superior man*
*stakes his life on following his will,*

and you always did that, follow your will,
that's what you taught me to do,
that's what I learned from you.

## Cracked Cup

You serve me tea
in a cracked cup,
does that mean
you want to break up
with me?

## Blake In America

When I open my suitcase,
Blake hops out,
a tiny mannequin not much bigger than a Ken doll,
with each breath he takes he grows larger,
until we stand eye to eye.
He is round-shouldered, potbellied,
stiff white whiskers on his face, like an old cat,
he doesn't look happy,
*Where is the shitter*, he howls,
his breath smells of garlic and cheese,
I lead him into my bathroom,
show him the commode,
when I demonstrate the flushing mechanism,
he jumps back startled.
*Beezelbub!* he cries, *I know Satan's roar,*
*I will not thrust my arse into his jaws.*
I tell him he is in the twenty-first century now,
I have no outhouse; this is the New World,
I point out the roll of toilet paper,
leave him, close the door.
I continue unpacking.
Soon, I hear the toilet flush,
Blake comes out standing straighter,
*I have relieved myself in the Lake of Albion*, he sings
*but where is the gentle shore, the surround of trees,*
*the sturdy elm, oak and willow,*
*where the hummingbird, the ladybugs, the bees?*

Where indeed?

# Come Poem

I come, smelling of joy, clean as a pearl,
watching Neal Armstrong walk on the moon on TV,
I see my future as a series of outer worldly embraces,
imploding explosions within near and far galaxies of
     shimmering skin.

I come, squealing, in a bedroom on Avenue D,
smoking morning glory seeds mixed with scrapings
from the inside of a banana peel,
I come through decades marked with the assassinations of
     visionaries,
I come in years of plague, even when I practice safe sex,
I'm afraid, but I come.

I come in melancholy and loneliness
although I may not be coming alone,
I come until I start writing poems,
I come after I start writing poems,
I try not to think about poems when I'm coming but
that's not something I can always control.

I come into the first century of a new millennium,
I orgasm in times of farcical immoral government, faux, mass-
     market spirituality,
desperate consumer consumption, crippling poverty, intense
     private despair,
I come floating up into the air like a prayer,
I come because coming is still a revolutionary act.

I come everywhere; I come in my ears listening to Hayden's
     *Horn Concerto #2,*
I come listening to Charlie Parker's sax play *Bird in Paradise.*
I come shouting clichés like: give it to me baby, give it to me
     baby - Oh, Oh, Oh,
or I come whispering so low not even my partner will hear me

the name of a God I profess not to believe in,
I come growing rosebuds from my navel,
I come riding the A train, covered in good news,
I come shitting and pissing,
I come because I want to come,
I come because you want me to come
I come because I can only go for broke
or I won't come at all,
I come playing an imaginary violin,
all my strings, tight, tuned and ready,
I come for you.

# Night

Loose as a goose
after Feldenkrais class
I move down
Sixth Avenue,
my happiness
clumsy and quacking,
somewhere around
Bed, Bath & Beyond,
I mutate into
another species
capable of flight,
my heart grows wings,
rises into the night.

# Join

*(for Elizabeth Murray*
*[1940–2007]*
*inspired by her painting* Join *[1980])*

If color is a function of feeling,
you felt the world in your fingers
every time you picked up a brush,
Elizabeth Murray, with your wonder-wheeling colors,
leaping like fireworks into solar nebulaes,
into lunar lexicons, into glimmering galaxies,
flying asteroids of wild-wheeling feelings!
What colors, Elizabeth Murray! What trilling,
thrilling, swinging singing, wing-a-dings of wonder and heart!

Elizabeth Murray, you are off the chart
with your persuasive pinks, pinker then the pinkest peonies,
pink as the flower between Kwan Yin's legs,
pink as a posse of piglets, pink as the eternal feminine,
pink as the first flush of attraction, before the fear reaction sets in,
and your greens, your greens, give me hope, Elizabeth Murray,
your Gatorade greens, Robin Hood greens,
greens for the heart center which the Yogis say is the home of love,
your greens are green as Lorca's green ship on the green sea,

I must not forget your reds, Elizabeth Murray,
reds sultry as the steamy kiss of sex,
ripe tomato reds, subversive hammer and sickle reds,
gallant fire engine reds, bubbling burgundy reds,
deep garnet reds growing into purple,
purple -- the pluperfect union of blue and red, cold and hot,
purple the color of passion and forget-me-nots.

I could spend forever talking about your romance with colors,
Elizabeth Murray, your yarrow yellows, beaming blues,
your glowing oranges, glistening as the rising sun,
but I want to tell you how free your art makes me feel,
how it brings me wheelbarrows filled with wit and grace,
how it embroiders my inner and outer space,
Elizabeth Murray.

## Belly Of The Beast

I saw my old Yoga teacher on the street,
holding hands with a woman who looked
like Paris Hilton,
he was wearing Manolo Blahniks on his feet,
he had gained twenty pounds at least,
how voracious is the belly of the beast,
how hungry.

# No Surrender

My father sounds weak on the phone,
*Sure, honey,* he says, *I'm okay,*
his voice fading away,
*I'm doing the best I can,* he tells me.

He likes to say this is the family motto,
but it is not my motto,
my motto is *No Surrender.*

Yet I wonder how I'll feel when
I can't use a walker anymore,
have to use a wheelchair,
sleep in a bedroom that always
smells of urine and Vapo-Rub,
what kind of poems will I write then.
I will be too crippled by anger
to pick up a pen and write *No Surrender.*

There are signs his best is not good anymore,
he wheels out to the lobby to get his mail
and when he comes back into his apartment
forgets to lock the door,
One night at 3 a.m. he wakes his neighbors,
he's in the hall, doing wheelies in his chair,
yelling *I'm a robot, I'm a robot.*

When told about his behavior
the next morning, he weeps.

**Gitmo**

I' m lying in bed watching McNeil-Lehrer,
I'm waiting for the egg,
it's already boiling in the water but
I don't want to take it out before it is time
and ruin the salad with a runny yolk.

The face of the first Gitmo prisoner to be tried
in Federal court comes on the screen,
he doesn't look like a terrorist,
he looks like a sweetheart,
big doe eyes, mouth like an angel
young, clean-shaven, no Al Quaeda beard,
but is anything ever what it seems…

Tomorrow I go to the hospital for tests,
I feel fine but what about the bleeding,
a brief aberration or an indication
of something deeper, something foul.

I shopped carefully for the salad,
French feta from Sahadi's,
premium olive oil from the health food store,
organic spinach, carrots, scallions,
the perfect ripe avocado,
even the lemon is organic just like I am
with my porous aging bones,
working kidneys, liver and spleen,
it's the uterus I'm worried about,
long retired but maybe bored now,
cantankerous, acting up,
at least my lungs are fine,
I had an x-ray last month,
and an MRI, my heart is well,
a sturdy pump,
a heart that can dance,

a heart that can love,
but it is strong enough to carry me away
from the river Styx
back to the lake of my days...

*Timing is every thing*, Luis said
last month in the bar, I agreed,
and then he kissed me,
we didn't do so well after that,
was it him or me that fumbled the pass?
What does it matter?

When Lehrer starts to sum up the news,
I know the egg is ready, I go to the kitchen,
crack the egg against the sink,
peel it under cold water, like my mother taught me,
she also taught me to knock wood when I am afraid,
I knock the oak tabletop three times,
I sit down to eat; I look out the window,
day is gone, night has got the world in his teeth,
the salad couldn't be better.

# Tantalus

Whenever I hold love in my hand,
it slips through my fingers like ebb tide,
not a drop left to wet my parched lips,
my thirsty body cracks from the inside,
my veins run dry,
what did I do to deserve this torture,
steal divine food from the
table of the gods, what did I do,
cut up my young son and serve him in a stew...

Was I a con artist in another life,
or Mr. Goodbar or a rock star who used
her lovers like toilet paper?

Did I let my neediness seep through
leaving ugly stains all over you,
did I try to take control,
assume the mother role,
iron your shirts, cook your food,
because I was afraid of letting go
afraid to surrender to the ebb and flow...

I wander around my room
like a tragic heroine in some
old Alfred Lord Tennyson poem,
I try to remember your face, but it fades away
back into the dark lake of memory,
I try to follow after you, down, down, down,
I fall in the mud, I drown.

# Snowed In

Snowed in on this third day of February,
still hung over from two nights ago at the bar,
I drank half of Yuko's Irish Coffee
plus three sakes while flirting
with that guy with the funny hat,
maybe he was the pope,
now even reading Bukowkski doesn't comfort me
so I turn on Channel 7 at four o'clock
and I'm just another sad, lonely lady
watching Oprah,
how did this happen?

# Ubiquitous Blake

Blake explores New York on his own,
walks over the Brooklyn Bridge, takes snapshots with his third
    eye,
grabs on to the back of the # 41 Bus, rides to Central Park,
where he climbs a high tree and surveys the scene:
the boaters on the lake, the picnics on the grass,
dogs bark, frisbees fly through the air,
babies ride in strollers pushed by adoring grown-ups,
pretty girls in bright dresses walk together talking and laughing,
*Heaven on earth*, Blake exclaims,
he begins to sing, *when the meadows laugh with lively green,*
until the police come, make him get down from the tree.
They want to take him to a homeless shelter,
he tells them he is not homeless, he is my houseguest,
says my name is Marie Antoinette, gives them my phone
    number,
so they let him go.

Blake digs though the garbage for bottles to redeem,
earns enough to buy a backpack from a peddler on Thirty-Third
    Street
and an assortment of shoe polish at Duane Reade,
he opens for business outside Grand Central Station,
the other bootblacks give him a hard time, tell him he can't
    work
there because he isn't part of the union.
He argues, says he has heard this kind of talk before,
but, finally, he wanders uptown,
sets up outside the Metropolitan Museum of Art
where he attracts many customers who tell him he looks
like the portraits inside by Rembrandt.

Blake goes to a candle light vigil for peace in Union Square,
he walks around lighting other people's candles with his own,

a retired social worker from the Bronx is intrigued,
she asks him where he is from, he says *kingdom come,*
asks him what he does; he says he is *a traveler on the road,*
she sighs, charming as he is, he is not for her she concludes,
he is missing a few screws, but at least, seems harmless.

# Tiger Of Desire

After twenty years,
I get an e-mail from you,
in London,
you say you have been
thinking of me,
of our great times together,
it would be nice to see me.
I write right back,
I've been thinking of you too,
if you're ever in New York,
please come visit.
I give you my unlisted
phone number.
In my mind I see you leave her,
coming to live with me,
see us sharing an orange,
see your arms close around me,
rocking me against your chest
like a baby,
I don't hear the tiger creep up,
don't know he is behind me,
until his claw sinks into my shoulder,
the pain like razors
cutting though my heart,
bleeding out into my fingers
on the keyboard,

Memories are raw meat for this tiger,
such a fat tiger, so obese,
what a belly, bloated with fantasies,
I can feel his heat behind me,
his greedy breath at my neck,
that does not stop me
from ending my letter,
*Forever yours......*

## Irwin's Eyes

Irwin was a humble person,
he studied Buddhism,
he was my next-door neighbor,
when he came to visit
he took off his shoes
outside the door because he
didn't want to dirty my floor.
A couple of Irwin's photos were in MOMA
but he drove a taxi, owned
three shirts, two pairs of pants,
a ragged black leather jacket and
the Leica he used to take pictures
of naked women bathing in waterfalls,
old couples walking together
on the streets of New York.

Irwin's eyes were holy,
he saw the heart of things,
he saw life opening and closing,
he was depressed about Vietnam,
Watergate, about how we, his neighbors,
quarreled, didn't trust each other,
he started taking color slides,
roaming Brooklyn Streets
to capture a cracked blue plaster Jesus
in someone's garbage,
a gray spirit nest of half-smoked cigarettes
in a snow-covered garden.

Irwin jumped out his window
the first day of Spring 1974,
he was thirty-nine,
his last words before he died in the gutter were
*we are all guilty.*

Did he find Buddha's bliss on the other side
or an infinite abyss, dark as the inside of a camera?

Last year Irwin was discovered
through a website his brother Alan set up
by a rich man who owned a gallery
so Irwin had a Madison Avenue show.
The opening was on a Friday night
between Passover and Easter,
the room was too small,
the pictures too close together on the wall,
the wine too sweet, it didn't matter,
Irwin was there inside every frame,
proof of how the soul can survive the body.

In the catalogue notes the owner of the gallery
said nothing about Irwin's suicide,
his death was described as a tragic fall,
Alan, now indexing the final slides,
thinks his brother knew he would die
in Brooklyn, his death thus premeditated,
the slides photo-journaling his suicide,
maybe Alan is right, who am I to say no,
but Irwin was always walking a high wire
between heaven and hell, maybe a giant black bird,
a carrion crow, pushed him and he fell.

# Dalachinsky's Collages

Dalachinsky's collages are hodgepodges of Hera and the Swan,
Vulcan at the forge, ecstatic Paris Boulevards
where a black glove reaches sky high for a red star,
mazes of color, yellows, purples, greens,
a sabre tooth tiger and Picasso illuminata convene
to form a free jazz scene while a lonely saxophone
blows serene as a buttercup.

Dalachinsky's collages are randy as an Iberian Ibex,
idealistic as a car wreck, idiosyncratic as a turkey neck,
indefinable (though I'm trying to find words for them
in this poem), indelible, incandescent as a thousand watt bulb,
a blue sailor boy in short pants shows his back,
a musician plays bass with Giacometti fingers,
images linger like the shadow of a lily pad on the pond of
        despond.

Dalachinsky's collages put the yellow cockette on Napoleon's
        fancy hat,
joust with Emily Dickenson's existential lace,
jump into Walt Whitman's young clean-shaven face,
(I thought he was Woody Guthrie),
Dalachinsky's collages journey up the Boulevard Voltaire,
down the Boulevard Diderot to the land of you never know,
you never know, you never know, you never know.

# At Coney Island On My Birthday

On his high white chair,
in billowing saffron shorts
a skinny young life guard stands,
like a Buddha protecting me
from the capricious ocean,
the oblivion of the sands.

# Lebanon

Above us, even now, the same stars
the priest-astronomers saw
glitter and revolve like pinwheels,
the moon will be full tonight,
I read it in this morning's Daily News
along with the reports of yesterday's casualties
and the massacre in Tibron.
We used to kid around about
how we solved the Arab-Israeli conflict,
that was twenty-five years ago.
I wonder if you ever think of me,
I remember the night I followed you to the water's edge,
*My country was once the Paris of the East* you said,
and pulled me down to lie with you beside the timeless sea.

# New York Post Poem

*(January 4, 2008)*

Today, January 4, 2008, the New York Post tells us about the
mob plot to kill Rudy, (if one more capo had voted yes, Guiliani
would never have had another chance to put on a dress), Gwen
Stefani has nice legs, 48% of Americans more stressed out now
then in the last five years, Code Pink protestor, name withheld,
waves her hands, which were covered in faux blood, in the face
of Condoleezza Rice at Foreign Affairs committee meting, calls
Rice a war criminal, the Preppy Killer is in a jailhouse fog after
drug bust, *I don't know what's happening* he says, subway fare
hike is on a fast track, eighty-nine year old actor killed in Upper
East Side Hit and Run while going out to buy the doorman
of his building coffee, Perdue fully cooked chicken nuggets
are $3.99 at Gristede's while Ben and Jerry's, assorted varieties
are two for six dollars, tonight will be mostly cloudy 47 to 52
degrees and Libra natives are told this: Something you spent
days, weeks, maybe even months worrying about will reveal
itself to be of no importance at all over the next twenty-four
hours. The simple fact is that you allowed your imagination to
get the better of you and ended up visualizing all sorts of trials
and terrors that did not exist.

# Jerry in Assisted Living

My father's world has gotten smaller.
It is now the size of a ten by twelve room
in an assisted living facility
in Millersville, Maryland.

Outside the two windows he can
see a tree, a patch of grass
and a piece of today's gray winter sky.

He is sitting in his wheelchair,
I am sitting on the bed,
having just spent half-an-hour
trying to show him how to push the
button down on the can of
Axe spray deodorant,
he insisted on this brand because
he saw it on television,
he can barely move his fingers,
like his feet, now crippled by neuropathy.
*I can't do this*, he says, *I'm too old.*

Tears fill his eyes, his head lolls on his chest
like a marionette with a torn string,
then he looks up, at his closet without a door,
on the only shelf sit three baseball caps,
instead of the twenty he used to own.

He asks me for the navy blue one,
with the DC letters for the DC Nationals,
*Put it on me*, he asks, at first I do it wrong,
*No, no*, he shouts, *don't pull the brim down*,
I try again, this time I get it right.
Cap perched jauntily on the back of his head,
he sits up straighter, now he is Jerry the Sport.

He grabs the telephone on the table by the bed,
calls his offshore betting account.
Somewhere in Costa Rica or Ecuador
a woman answers, I can hear her voice,
her Spanish accent, she takes his bet for the
Ravens/Steelers game, Ravens by three points,
and for the space of a New York minute,
makes my father happy again.

## Blake At Brighton Beach

I want to escape national politics, Blake wants to escape
      religious zeal,
so we decide to go to Brighton Beach.
On the D train, surrounded by noisy families,
children drumming their plastic pails, teen lovers with pierced
      lips,
old folks with hearing aids and canes,
Blake sits, solid as an obelisk in the middle of a battlefield.
He gnaws a spare rib from last night's Chinese take-out,
hiccups and spits, a hunk of gristle lands at my feet,
obscene as the butt of a cigarette,
I cover it with my sneaker, wonder if the other
passengers will think he is my father or even worse, my date.

On the beach, we settle at waters edge,
Blake won't share the blanket, refuses my sunscreen,
takes off his shirt to reveal a flabby chest,
powerful, muscled arms like Hercules.
In his worn, brown velvet pantaloons he kneels, seizes a broken
      shell,
starts to draw angels in the wet sand,
I go for a swim, paddle in the lovely salty brine
to an isle of beginner's mind, a far paradise where anything is
      possible.
I want to tell Blake how great the water is,
but when I get back to our spot, he is not alone,
a zoftig blonde in a black string bikini crouches beside him,
her buttocks fat, fluffy clouds,
she is holding a cigarette in crimson talons,
*You do not have a match*, she speaks, in a Russian accent,
*but do you have the time?*
Blake replies: *The hours of folly are measured by the clock.*
She looks perplexed but does not give up.
*Come with me under the boardwalk,*

*I'll show you my angel*, she coaxes,
Blake puts down the shell, rises,
*The lust of the goat is the bounty of God,* he cries,
off they go, leaving me
to contemplate the marriage of sea and sky.

# Love Is A Virago, Rimbaud

Love is a virago, Rimbaud,
a runaway train with a mind of
its own, it speeds past my stop,
takes me where I didn't want to go,
when the temperature goes up
it melts away like the angels
I used to make in the snow.
My love is too often imagined,
absurd, absent like a stunt man beside
me in bed with a boner as big as
a slide trombone,
love is my addiction, my sustaining affliction,
a storm of pleasure and pain,
that makes me understand Rimbaud,
why you spent all your time hanging out
with Verlaine.

My love is radiant, like in radiation poisoning,
rosy and rash like the measles,
multi-colored like a hallucinating kaleidoscope,
sticky, gummy, held together by tricky goo,
Rimbaud, like the opium you and Verlaine
smoked with your friend De Quincy,
no matter how hard you pinch me,
the dream of love is one
from which I don't ever want to wake up,
even if love is a virago,
a buttercup filled with fool's gold,
it's still dope, Rimbaud, it's still dope.

# Low Life

The Low Life low life got me where I am today,
stained sheets, sweaty smells of skin on skin,
cigarette butts in the dregs of the gin,
transient jobs, waitress, chambermaid,
too stoned, disconnected,
shabby, crabby to apply
for a job that was better paid,
a life that was better paid,
whole weeks when all I could afford to eat
was a daily pint of
take-out roast pork fried rice,
paradise was half a night of drugged sleep
with no dreams.

I don't know how exactly
I made my way out
into the world
where I live now,
a world where at least sometimes,
light pierces the darkness,
but I know the low life
put the words in my mouth
to make this poem,
the lowlife stitched
into my bones
like barbed wire.

# Morocco

Richard was behind the bar
so I didn't have to pay for drinks,
he said he'd give me a ride home
if I stuck around till closing,
I was feeling fine by the time
Red came in, yesterday when I
was visiting my connection,
I met him, he had long fingers,
a nasty mouth, he kept looking at my legs.

The seat next to me was empty, he took it,
offered to buy me a drink, I said no
but he still inched closer, bold like I like them.
I could smell the tobacco on his breath
and something stronger, darker, maybe opium,
you could get it in those days,
he started talking about Coleridge and Baudelaire,
like he knew I was a poet though I hadn't said,
he asked me to come to his place, get high,
I said I was waiting for a ride,
*Aw, come on*, he said, *it's only a block away,
just for a while,*
I told Richard I'd be back,
he knew how I was, he didn't bat an eye.

I was right about the opium,
we smoked it in a silver pipe he said was from Tangier,
then Red turned out the lights, lit candles,
it was night time in Morocco,
the smell of oranges floated in the air,
he bent me over a low chair, pulled down my panties,
fingers hot on my ass coaxing, opening,
he used me like a boy, I didn't care. I liked it.

We smoked another bowl, he wanted
to go to the bar, have another drink
I told him I'd see him around.
Outside, the streetlights were burning like fire,
a crescent moon danced over Second Avenue,
I made it back to the bar just in time.

# Crazy Stuff

I dream, hear whispers,
memories in the night,
crazy stuff, like what you
used to say to me,
*Come on baby, open wide,*
*can't you take it deeper,*
*you don't know how to use that thing,*
then louder than your voice
I hear thunder in the sky,
the hum-hum-hum of the cars on the bridge,
tires screech to a sudden stop,
I open my eyes to dust and shadow,
there you are standing somewhere
at the edge of the room,
as the sunlight filters in,
you fade,
particulate,
evaporate,
are gone.

# Here She Is

I call my father Sunday night at the
assisted living home in Millersville, Maryland,

*Well,* he says when he picks up the phone,
*she's been waiting for your call all day*

*Who has been waiting for my call?* I want to know

*Your sister,* he tells me, *she is right here*
*lying next to me,*

I realize he thinks I am my mother's older sister Mildred,
dead since 1987, who used to call on Sundays,
and he thinks my mother, gone ten years, is lying beside him

*So,* he says, *don't you want to speak to her?*
*Sure* is all I can manage,
*then okay,* he says, *here she is*
and hangs up the phone.

# Blake's Crabby Hand

I wake up on my birthday morning,
on the pillow next to me
is a note written in Blake's crabby hand:

*The winds of night carry me*
*into clouds of fire,*
*my respite here was filled with*
*new experience, inspiration for my songs,*
*your hospitality warmed my cold spirit,*
*you kept honey in your pantry,*
*brewed fine coffee,*
*shared your gin with me*
*and that Russian schnapps*
*called Smirnoff, I found very tasty,*
*the floor in your kitchen*
*is covered with grime*
*but the linens you gave me for*
*my bed were fresh and smelled like apples.*
*You struggle with your wanton nature,*
*aspire to be a fine lady,*
*take pains with your appearance,*
*make effort to spread good cheer,*
*ninny girl, you are not so foolish*
*as you first appear,*
*you burn too hot*
*but flame bright and true*
*I wish you long, happy life.*
*Farewell,*
> *Your friend,*
> *William Blake*

# Hot Water

Small minds find dirt everywhere,
hair trapped on the computer screen,
dust motes floating in the air.
I try for an open mind,
search for the window of
opportunity in the coffee grinds,
I want to see the big picture.
I don't find it in our empty wine glasses,
that bottle of red must have cost you forty bucks,
you apologize for being so out of touch
for so many years,
you say I was your best friend back then,
*Why did you abandon me,* I blurt out,
after a pause, you shrug,
*It won't happen again,* you say,
you have a diamond in one of your front teeth,
I don't mention it but I wonder if
I'm wearing too much make-up,
you look so sleek and happy, still with her
after thirty years, your daughters grown now,
your gold wedding band thick as my tongue,
I try to pretend I'm satisfied with my life,
I wonder if you know it's a charade.
after you leave, I take the glasses to the sink,
turn on the faucet, wait for the water to heat,
I wash the glasses under hot water.
I dry them. I put them away.

# Springtime

She watches him play basketball,
Spring is when the game heats up,
the ball hitting the wall
sounds like a cork popping,
the juice of love runs in the streets,
women wear short skirts
to show off their knees,
pussy willows, daffodils, peonies
for sale outside the delis,
peonies make me think of romance,
how the many pink petals open to
reveal a purple heart,
peonies make me want a lover,
make me want my body
opening into summer heat.

Her gaze lingers on the strong arc
of his arm as he raises it
when the palm of his hand
connects with the ball,
he slams it so hard and fast
his opponent doesn't have a chance,
she purses her lips, throws him a kiss,
he looks over at her in time to catch it.

After the game he buys her an ice cream cone.

# Addis Ababa

Crooked hills of Addis Ababa,
damsels playing dulcimers,
wild Abyssinian forests,
dark inland rivers Juba and Dawa,
kettle drums, sohrgum, tobacco and barley
surround me, rising up from this cup
of organic Ethiopian coffee
brewed from beans I got last week
at Porto Rico Coffee and Tea
on Bleecker Street.

# Equinox

autumn begins,
the earth shifts,
my spirit drifts
like falling leaves
down the river,
my heart floats
in my thin skin boat
towards winter,
what to leave,
what to keep,
the trees weep,
the earth is a rush
of wind and water.

# Before The Election

On a rainy morning on Stanton Street
a pregnant girl stands under the awning of
the bodega in a ratty black coat
that no longer buttons,
her belly holds the future of America,
an empty Marlboro pack floats in the gutter,
silver foil shines like the flash of a knife,
what America will her child know,
an America made by hippies who traded
their copies of *Be Here Now*
for gold Visa Mastercards,
an America of stone soup, rice and beans,
prayers to a virgin dead two thousand years...

Flacco and Johnny turn the corner,
Flacco holding a joint cupped in his hand,
he passes it to Johnny,
Johnny cradles it between his
palms like Aladdin's lamp,
takes a hit, *Obama's the man* he says,
*Fuckin' A* says Flacco

A few steps away, the young mother
doesn't hear them,
she is listening deep inside herself
as a tiny hand unfurls,
matchstick fingers reach up towards the world.

## Dirty Dancing

The Daily News says Patrick Swayze died yesterday,
pancreatic cancer at age 57,
I turn the page and read about Queens terror raids,
Feds search apartments in Flushing for the Al Quaeda
version of the Koran, manuals on making bombs.

I'm more afraid of cancer, the other great terror
of our age, an aberration on an X- ray,
a constellation of tiny terror cells,
when I found that lump in my back,
I went crazy until the biopsy showed it was renegade fat,
biopsy, colonoscopy, mastectomy, hysterectomy,
I hate these words, spreading fear
everywhere like greenhouse gas,
we breathe it in like oxygen,
fear, the monster plague no one escapes,
fear of death, and all her little ones,
disease, malaise, dementia, failure,
loneliness, fear of falling trees, fear of intimacy,
in the bar Luis says me he loves me but
he doesn't want us to become any more involved
because he is afraid he will be unfaithful.

I lay awake in bed at night curled into a knot of anxiety,
what will happen to me,
when what I want is to run away to the Catskills and
dance with Patrick Swayze,
I listen for his music in the air but it's not there.

# Rackety Old Jack

*(for Jack Michiline)*

Rackety Old Jack,
three steps forward,
four steps back,
could crack a poem across
the page like greased lightening,
solitary old crow, ringing
my spirit telephone to remind me
*Be yourself, be yourself,*
*be yourself forever,*
*caw, caw, caw...*

# Lily Of The Valley

In the summer when I was little
we went to a bungalow in the Catskills,
taking my hand my mother led me through
the piney woods that were all around,
teaching me to know the flowers,
pink mountain laurel grows in clumps,
orange Jack-in-the-pulpit sticks out a black tongue
thin as the point of a pencil,
lily of the valley was her favorite,
fragile white bells swing on a leafy green string.

So many years later, in the midst of a heat wave,
I drift like a weed through rank city gutters, steamy and vast,
but her cool fingers curl over mine, holding fast.

**True Believer**

I'm doing Yoga like a true believer,
a Mennonite, a holy roller, a wistful fool
who still believes in the Ten Commandments,
I'm doing yoga to masturbate with no hands,
because my ego and my id don't correspond,
my libido is a fat fish trapped in a skinny pond,
I'm tired of walking around
with a begging bowl between my legs
I want to stretch into a new dimension,
a place where grace beats karma.

I don't want to run after love,
the peace I need is in my own body,
if anywhere at all, so I'm doing yoga
with a weeks worth of garbage in the hall
while the earth turns on its axis beneath me,
the deli on the corner sells the first daffodils,
a bunch for $1.79,
I do yoga to grow daffodils in my mind,
psychotherapy takes too many lifetimes,
I don't want to burn up with desire,
I want to let my passions simmer
on a slow fire,
I want to find the needle on my compass,
I want the best wine in my glass
so I do warrior pose, I do the shooting bow,
the eagle, the turtle, the tree,
I do yoga, I open my heart,
I flex my feet.

## Jerry In Dementia

There are locks on all the windows here
because they are afraid you will crawl
out towards the sun.

Your last days will be lit by
flickering images on TV-on-off-on,
you are like that now-on-off-on,
nodding in your wheel chair
like a crazy king on a throne.

The nurse told me yesterday
she found you sitting there
wearing your yarmulke,
your pants down,
when she said *lunch is ready*,
you said *leave me the fuck alone.*

Today I came to tell you I love you
and I always will
but no one can find your hearing aid
and you can't hear a word I say.

# Rising Sun Howl Poem

I howl for the rising sun
that puts the mama jam in the bim-bam,
the mojo in the yoyo, the song in the lingo,
the drumbeat in the ringo, the jelly in the roll,
the o-o-o-o- in the riotous, desirous soul,
I howl in praise of every hair in Allen Ginsberg's nose,
I howl because demon oil is now the cosmic toad,
I howl because my heart is always on the road,
I howl to appease the demons of my unmanageable ego,
but it never works,
I howl in praise of the temple of the body,
the only true church and in praise of the stink of love,
raisin-y and bittersweet come drying on the sheet,
I howl in praise of Bob Holman's feet and in
praise of the days when the hangover is worth it.

I howl for the displaced, mutilated, slaughtered, the freaks,
the lonely, the pretenders, the dead enders, the lost,
the poets who constantly imitate Robert Frost,
I howl for all our power failures especially our
inability to love one another,
I howl because the dew is still wet on my petunia,
I howl in prayer to the Big Breasted Buddha of Congenial
     Union,
I howl in joy because I live for the power of the word.
Poetry makes my self-consciousness fly away with big bird,
I howl for poetry, hully-gully bumblebee, banshee, calliope,
sweet pea, blue sea, Sancho Panza-Don Quixote,
Lao-Tse, Comanche remedy for deceit and misery,
at least temporarily.
I howl for every roll of the dice,
I howl for brown rice, alpha rays and runaways,
I howl for foreplay.

# Surprise Party

Love catches me unexpecting
like a surprise party
with many balloons,
he helps me on
with my sweater,
pizza never tasted
this good.

## The Arrow Is The Soul

Doing yoga on my belly
on the kitchen floor,
I grab my ankles with my hands,
lift into bow pose,
the arrow is the soul,
I rock back and forth
like a metronome,
long life my goal
even though I know
it's a crap shoot.

I try to get the breathing right,
inhale forward, exhale back,
I rush it, go too fast,
too anxious to succeed,
to seize control,
when what I need is
to surrender to all possibilities,
what I need is to learn at William Blake's knees,
good thing they didn't elect me president.

I arch my back into locust pose,
it stimulates my brain,
I look down my nose at infinity,
breathe long, deep and slow,
long, deep and slow, again and again,
breathing in the winds of time,
Mother Earth, the deep sublime,
long, deep and slow,
long, deep and slow,
I keep at it until I let go,
let go, let go
and fly off the wheel of blame,
embrace my miserable history,

forgive everyone, even myself.
How did it happen – Holy Moly!
It's a miracle!

First sunny day in a week and
I'm going to the beach,
How did this happen- it's a miracle!
Holy Moly! Holy Moly! Holy Moly!

## Utopia Poem

In my utopia, cunnilingus will be considered free speech,
my wazoo will play the kazoo,
my grasp will not exceed my reach,
my crotch will never smell like the blues,
my ass will be the pride of Brooklyn
and firm as a not quite ripe peach.
I will be a six-foot tall Amazon princess
giving out free cotton candy at the beach
or a fighter pilot whose one target
is the closed mind.
I will never be waiting for someone who isn't coming
or coming for someone who isn't waiting.
Compassion will be the only true religion,
all body types will be fashionable,
public officials will get enemas twice a week.

In my utopia, *He-done-me-wrong* poetry, *She-done-me-wrong*
     poetry,
any kind of victimization poetry, will be replaced
by poetry that colonizes the moon,
the fragile heart of life will be protected by a cocoon
woven from the love of truth,
Neil Young will be our shepherd,
Crazy Horse will never die,
Confucius will write all the fortunes
in the fortune cookie factory,
purple satin corsets will hold up the sky,
Mommy and Poppy will always be there to
take us for motorcycle rides,
in my utopia breathing will get you high,
I will always be yours and you will always be mine.

# Lament

you came to
see me after
fifteen years
and I didn't
have any coffee in
the house
or any beer

where did
the last roll
of toilet paper go,
how could
the paper towels
be gone also...

# The Seed Of Blake

I dream of Blake today,
his seed is in my head,
bursting its skin,
elegant thought reaching
out with tiny roots,
seeking ground within,
*Infinity is in love with the productions of time,*
says Master William.

I do yoga, I do plough pose, cobra,
I stretch my bones and hear them crack
like twigs under the devil's boot,
I strain to hear the rhythm
beneath the words I write,
if I could hear the song
of the spheres as they turn
on a beam of light
then I would be like the man
sweeping the interpreter's parlor,
I would be like Milton finding paradise
or the Queen of Heaven in Glory,
(here maybe I am being too grandiose),
but I keep at it, I do warrior pose, I do crow,
I stand on my head hoping
Blake will take form inside my dark mind
and bend it back like a bow.

# New Year's Eve

Refreshments were knishes from Yonah Schimmel's,
champagne sparkled like a holy spring,
the New Year came in dancing at the Living Theater,
high stepping to the music of the spheres,
free styling, world wheeling Baba Israel got us there,
Solomon and Sheba whirled around us,
weaving passion flowers in the air,
at midnight there were so many hugs and kisses
no one was a stranger,
holding hands in a circle,
We joined in a gigantic OOOm
like the hum of bees in a hive
intent only on sweetness.

# Matthew Shipp Plays Piano At Tribes Gallery

A giant egg
cracks over our heads,
thunder and lightening,
out from the piano keys
the ship tosses the storm,
worlds tremble,
oceans crest and curl,
Africa splits at the equator,
Kilimanjaro rises, falls
into the raging sea of relentless sorrow,
hurricane winds blow out the windows, the doors,
he makes my confession for me,
playing an old upright on East Third Street,
sewer rats become serpents,
glide up into the ragged trees,
a motley Eden but it's something,
Matt's fingers lawless symphonies,
the line of his back as he sits
on the piano bench graceful as a willow,
the air clears,
it smells like salt.

## Cleaning The Toilet

I don't even notice
the brown grit building up in the bottom of the bowl
until it looks like the black hole of all my sins,
a build-up of lies, evasions,
the mixed messages I send out,
the excesses I take in,
that extra helping of kasha varniskes,
the spoons full of peanut butter I eat
straight from the jar at night when I can't sleep.

Then, this morning, as I'm standing up to flush
I see the crust of blackness at the bottom of my life,
see where I am going, down into the sewers with the alligators.

I grab the new toilet brush I got at Bed, Bath and Beyond
last week when the fear of death overwhelmed me so much
I had to buy something, anything, to prove I was still alive,
I'm out of Mr. Clean so I fling open the door to the cabinet
under the sink, get the bottle of Windex, take off the cap and
pour it all into the bowl and the water turns blue,
lapis lazuli blue, blue as the Nile, blue as perfect twilight,
blue as the eyes of a magical cat.

I get to work, scrub and scrub, working the brush
round and round, round and round, leaning into it,
bending my back, using my whole arm,
until the crud at the bottom of the bowl,
the blackness, the blackness, the blackness
begins to crack and float around in the bluey water
like pebbles, little pebbles getting smaller and smaller,
some of them small as a grain of sand.

# A Bird Singing In My Bathroom

There's a bird singing in my bathroom this morning,
I can hear it through the closed door,
there's a bird in my bathroom,
singing its heart out,
it must have flown in the open window
to escape the rain,
it's been snowing for days,
a cold January so far,
nothing but snow and dark skies,
as if the sun is afraid of something
but today, there is a bird singing in my bathroom,
a song as full of light as Sebastian's blue eyes,
a song as warm as the Caribbean,
as grand as the waves on the Sea of Japan,
a song to drive away the demons of the night,
a song louder than the rain,
a song strong enough to end all wars,
a song that cuts through
my terrors, my pain,
there's a bird singing in my bathroom,
singing a rhapsody,
there's a bird singing a rhapsody to somebody
and that somebody is me.

# From My Kitchen

From my kitchen I saw the sun set,
a great orange bubble
that fell slowly into the sea
behind the Statue of Liberty,
much later I saw the full moon
hang outside the window,
casting a yellow glow
into my room,
turning it to gold.

Such riches, even briefly, happiness,
despite the aching heart of the world,
the abominations, the cruelty, there is
still enough beauty to make this poem.

# Author's Note



*"Why do I write? What sin to me unknown dipt me in ink?*
*My parents, or my own?*

*Alexander Pope.*

My father's favorite poet was William Blake. His favorite poem was "Tyger," which he knew by heart. He would recite it to me when I was still in my crib. My mother loved Longfellow and used his poems to lull me to sleep. It is no wonder I always wanted to be a poet and wrote my first poem when I was seven. It was about a kachina doll I saw in the Broooklyn Museum. I chronicled my life and adventures in poems I wrote in my journals starting when I was ten but was too shy to share my poems with others. Not until I was in my mid forties did I find the courage to read my poems at open readings. I met other poets and entered the ever rich community of poetry. I never felt so alive. In 1992, Apathy Press published my first chapbook, *Pushing out the Envelope.* Since then I have had fifteen poetry chapbooks published, most recently, *Blue Blood of Morning*, Snapdragon Press 2009. Long Shot Press published *Baby On The Water*, my first full-length poetry collection, in 2003. My poems have appeared in over eighty publications including the New York Times, *Up Is Up But So Is Down, Bowery Women, A Gathering Of The Tribes, Paterson Literary Review, Long Shot, Wildflowers, Rattapallax, Curare, Outlaw Book Of American Poetry.* I have read my poems in over a hundred venues including the Howl Festival, Gathering Of The Tribes, Theater for the New City, St. Marks Church, Bowery Poetry Club, Nyorican Poets Café, National Arts Club. In 2004, I was an invited reader at Burning Tongues Poetry Festival in Ruigoord, Netherlands. I also write fiction, erotica, creative nonfiction, book reviews and art criticism. I wrote a play about Bukowski that premiered at the Bowery Poetry Club and had a successful run at FusionArts Museum. I have taught erotic writing and erotic literature at the New School, and Performance Poetry at the Bowery Poetry Club. Poetry is my heart, it propels me forward. I'm currently working on a chapbook of poems about my father. I feel my best work is ahead of me. I'm immensely happy Bowery Books has published *Cleaning The Duck* and hope whoever reads it finds pleasure.

CPSIA information can be obtained at www.ICGtesting.com
Printed in the USA
BVOW050058111111

275859BV00006B/4/P